To the two feminists
who are my
everything:
my mom, and my
daughter Riley

www.mascotbooks.com

Photography by Jeff Bartee Photography
Graphic Design by Jacqueline Kraft Design

For more information, please contact:
Mascot Books
620 Herndon Parkway, Suite 320
Herndon, VA 20170
info@mascotbooks.com

Library of Congress Control Number: 2018903421

CPSIA Code: PRT0718A
ISBN-13: 978-1-68401-963-2

Printed in the United States

F is for feminist

An A to Z Guide
for Feminists of All Ages

By Kim Collins

BE A **BOLD** girl

A Activism

Your voice and actions make a difference and can change the world!

B BOLD
Be a BOLD Girl!

C Choice

You decide your future.

D Dreams

Girls make their own

dreams come true!

E

Equality
Equal rights for all!

F Feminist

A person who supports equal rights and opportunities for women.

G

Glass Ceiling
Girls continue to break through barriers.

H

He can be a feminist too!

Everyone can be a champion of equality.

I International Day of the Girl

October 11 - A global movement to educate, protect, and empower girls.

J Justice
Because girls and women demand equality!

K Knowledgeable

Girls know that

Learning + Determination = Accomplishment

L

Leadership

Girls make
great leaders!

BE A BOLD GIRL

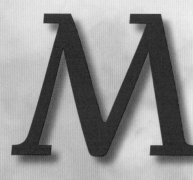

Mighty
Every girl has strength!

N Natural

Natural is beautiful.

O Our Bodies

We are the boss of our bodies.

P
Persist
Girls never give up!

Q Quiet?

Girls don't have to be quiet.
Use your voice!!

Every girl requires respect.

S.T.E.M.

Girls belong in science, technology, engineering, math, and anywhere else they want to be!

T Teamwork

Girls work together to get things done!

U Unique

Be yourself!
There is only one you.

V

Valuable

Girls add worth to the world!

W Wage Gap

Women earn less money than men for the same job. Does that make sense?

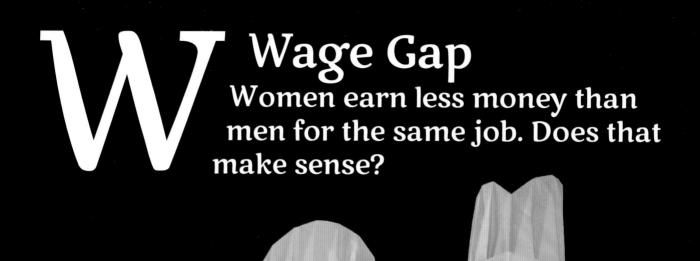

X

Title IX

A law that protects girls, so while you are in school you can learn, be safe, and play sports.

Y Yes we can!
Girls can do anything!

Z Zany

Girls can be all of these things and still have fun! So be BOLD! Enjoy your life, live your dreams, and don't let anything stop you from being the person you want to be!

ABOUT THE AUTHOR

Kim Collins lives in beautiful Belmont, California, with her husband; teenage daughter; dog, Finn; and cats, Ollie and Posey. Her son is away at college and she misses him every day. Her life is filled with women (beginning with her mom) who love and support her endlessly and inspire her daily. She has been writing for as long as she can remember and is living her dream by publishing her first book. Visit her online at beaboldgirl.com to say hello, ask a question, or check out the Feminist Starter Kit and other empowering and inspirational items.

Graphic Design by Jacqueline Kraft (jkraftdesign.com)
Photographs by Jeff Bartee Photography (jeffbartee.com)

ACKNOWLEDGMENTS

I would like to thank each of the BOLD girls who participated in the photo sessions for *F is for Feminist*. You are all fierce and awesome individuals, and I am so honored to include you in my book! My gratitude also extends to the amazing boys and adults, many of whom traveled several hours to participate.

Along those lines, to the many wonderful moms (and a few dads, an aunt, three grandmas, and two grandpas) who took a day off from work, left work early, had colleagues cover their shifts, took kids out of school (shhh!), sat in rush hour traffic for hours, worked around sick siblings, styled hair, picked out outfits, worked tirelessly and patiently with their children during their photo shoot (or had to leave the room because their child wouldn't stop looking at them instead of the camera), came on a moment's notice, helped me find other children to participate, and most of all, who trusted me with your most precious gifts: my sincere and heartfelt thanks for all you did for this book, and for all you do every day to raise feminists.

This book would not be what it is without the extraordinary talents of photographer Jeff Bartee (jeffbartee.com) and graphic designer Jacqueline Kraft (jkraftdesign.com). Jeff took my laughable sketches and turned them into a beautiful reality. Jacqueline took my vision and Jeff's photography and made magic happen, and followed with her relentless pursuit of perfection for the book as a whole. They both handled this project with passion and professionalism as if it were their own. I am forever grateful.

Special thanks to: Alina Vela (GoiaBoutique.com) for personally delivering her perfect handmade Rosie the Riveter headscarf for the "Yes We Can" photo shoot; Artist Courtney Carreras for her fabulous activist sign "Make Earth Cool Again" (facebook.com/Luna-Bay-Arts); Julie Delgado for taking the photograph of Samantha (jewelsphotographysite.com); at Mascot Books, Maria and Nina; and Anne Markle for your time, enthusiasm, and invaluable opinions.

Thank you to my mom, my family, and my village for your endless patience, encouragement, and input. Lastly, thank you to every one of the BOLD, feminist women in my life for being an inspiration! I love you all!!

xo, Kim

"Never, never, never give up. And remember to dance a little."
-Gloria Steinem

FEMINISM IS FOR EVERYONE.

Intersectional feminism includes all races, religions,
educations, genders, classes, sexualities, abilities, ages,
cultures, nationalities, languages, sizes, and more.

For a more detailed explanation of intersectional feminism,
please visit beaboldgirl.com.